The Nuts and Bolts of
PSYCHOLOGY
FOR
SWIMMERS

by Dr. Keith Bell

Library of Congress Cataloging-in-Publication Data

Bell, Keith F.
    Psychology for swimmers / by Dr. Keith Bell.
        p   cm.
    Summary: Discusses psychological methods of enhancing
    performance in swimming, covering such aspects as the
    challenge of training, goal setting, pain management, and
    handling pressure.
    ISBN 0-945609-00-0: $11.95
    1. Swimming — Psychological aspects. [1. Swimming —
    Psychological aspects.] I. Title.
GV838.53.P75B45   1980
797.2'101'9 — dc20   89-49231
                                                    CIP
                                                    AC

Photographic effects by William F. Jorn.

Printed in the United States of America.

10 9 8 7 6

This book is available at a special discount when ordered in bulk
quantities.

Published and distributed by:

Keel Publications
P.O. Box 160155
Austin, Texas 78716
(512) 327-1280
swimpair@flash.net

DEDICATION

To my parents, Jerry and Evelyn Bell, who sometimes
cared too much about my swimming, but who always cared.

CONTENTS

THE MAGIC PILL WITHIN

Competitive swimmers probably have made a greater commitment to their sport than any other group of athletes—amateur or professional. Swimmers train long hours at an incredible intensity. In addition, coaches have employed knowledge from exercise physiology, biomechanics and kinesiology to formulate training programs designed to strengthen, condition, and finely tune swimmers' bodies. They have their swimmers supplementing water work with running, yoga, weights, calisthenics, swim benches, shock cords, ropes, wheels, stretching and anything else that looks like it might help build strength, stamina and flexibility. In the water, swimmers are asked to further stress their capacity to perform work by using drag suits, donuts, paddles, tubes, stretch cords, wrist weights and the like. As a result, swimmers keep getting faster.

But everyone keeps getting faster. The technology is available to all. And most swimmers are training long hours at high intensity. Thus, competition has become more tightly contested at higher levels of performance.

Many races are so close that, if it were not for electronic timing systems, it would be nearly impossible to judge the outcome. It is not at all unusual to have eight finalists hit the finish within a few tenths of a second of each other. And often, there is virtually no difference in two competitors' times. In the 1972 Olympics, for example, Gunnar Larson won the 400 I.M. by two one-thousandths of a second over Tim McKee. And, believe it or not, some National Championships have been even closer. In 1975, Fred Tyler won the 200 I.M. at NCAAs in 1:50.628. Lee Engstrand also swam a 1:50.628 but the electronic timing system judged the race into the ten-thousandths of a second. In that race David Wilke was "way back" in third with a 1:50.67. That same year, the Women's 100 backstroke at AAUs was also decided by ten-thousandths of a second: Tauna Vandeweghe winning with a 58.128 over Nancy Garapick's identical 58.128.

Psychological considerations have always been integral factors in competitive swimming. But with the high uniformity of training, the tremendous physical investment in swimming universally made, and the resulting increasingly tight competitions: psychological factors have become even more important in determining the winner.

It is natural for the swimming community to look more and more toward psychology as a way to capture the winning edge. Unfortunately, too many swimmers and coaches are turning toward psychology, psychologists and motivational "experts" in search of a magic pill that will somehow, mysteriously, effortlessly and immediately charm their efforts into winning performances.

The magic is there. But it does not come mysteriously, effortlessly or immediately.

And too often the search for a magic pill is misdirected. Psychology has no magic pill to offer. Psychology can only help you find the magic pill within.

The magic lies within you. The human organism represents the greatest work of magic ever performed. Within you is the capacity to perform phenomenal feats. Your potential is limited only by your imagination and the commitment you are willing to make.

In this manual I present you with the nuts and bolts of psychology for swimming. I show you how to use good psychology to help you to get the most out of your training and to convert your preparation into the best possible meet performances. I offer no magic pill that effortlessly produces success. Rather, I show you how to release that magic pill within.

Like your physical training, the more you put into it, the more you get out of it. Good psychology is not mystical. It is straightforward. But it requires training, practice, and consistent, conscientious application. *You* must assume the responsibility for dragging out that magic pill from within, digesting it, and exploiting its power.

Go to it!

TRAINING

THE CHALLENGE OF TRAINING

Training is designed as a means to an end. Mainly, you train to enable you to swim as fast as possible in meets. The strength, endurance, flexibility, technical skill and psychological habits you build during practice largely determine how you perform in meets.

Training with the consistent intensity required to produce championship performances presents a formidable challenge. The day to day grind of two (sometimes three) a day practices, six or seven days per week all year round can find you tired, distracted and losing sight of what it is all about. The shadow of the routine easily obscures your view of where you are going. As a result, you may easily slip into going through the motions of training, carelessly wasting valuable opportunities and developing bad habits. You may begin to find unpleasant aspects in practice and dwell on them. You may start to think about *having to* be there and *having to* do various drills instead of wanting to. And subsequently you may find yourself eager to get it over with, looking for ways to avoid it and focusing on other things you might be doing instead.

All of this may be avoided with good psychology. You can make practices fun, meaningful, productive and satisfying. Let's see how.

GOAL SETTING

Set Goals

Competitive swimming is structured so that the object of the sport is to swim a particular stroke (or strokes, as in the I.M.) a designated distance faster than any of your competitors. Built around that goal are many standards and rewards that you might strive for: Olympic Championships, World Championships, National Team Trips, World Records, American Records, Conference Titles, State Championships, National Championships, All America teams, Top Ten Times, personal bests, etc. You may want to reach any or all of these goals. Most likely many of these will be important to you at various stages of your swimming career. In any case, you should designate goals that you can use to direct your training efforts. You need to make your intentions clear by setting goals.

Make A Commitment

Make a commitment to reach your goals and to do the training needed to get there. Put your goals down on paper. Writing them out helps to solidify a commitment.

A commitment is important. Once you have set a long term goal, you have decided to make the trip. Without a commitment, however, you are liable to question each step of the way.

Commit yourself to an intense training program. Don't allow yourself to be making decisions about whether to attend a given day's practice or whether to get after or cruise through the upcoming set. It doesn't make much sense to have to decide whether to take each individual step in a trip you have already decided to make.

Use Your Goals To Direct Your Training

Once you have set your sights on some goal, you should ask yourself: *"What is it going to take to reach my goal?"* If one of your goals is to make cut-offs for Nationals, it is relatively simple to determine what it will take. You need merely to look up this year's cut-off time for that particular event. If you aspire to make the Olympic team, final at Nationals, win the World Championships or another goal that depends on place rather than time, however, it is a little more difficult to specify exactly what you will need to go to accomplish your goal. Success will not only depend on what you do, but also on the efforts of others.-

You can never be certain of what others will do, but you and your coach can make a pretty good guess about what it would take to get where you want to go. Then, you can use that estimated time to set some goals for practice sessions. In this way, your goals can provide you with a blueprint for your training.

For instance, the example I used for the swimmers I worked with during the summer of 1980 was the goal of winning the Men's 200 m. butterfly at Long Course Nationals. At the time, the World Record was 1:59.23. I suggested that if I was interested in winning I would figure that someone was going to break the world record (and perhaps not just shave a few hundredths or tenths off of it). Thus, I would plan on having to go at least as fast as 1:57 to win.

Now, how would this direct my training? Well, if I wanted to go a 1:57 for a 200 m fly long course I would probably want to split a 56+ or 57 at the hundred and come back in 1:00 or 1:01. I would then use this information to direct my training. I would know, for example, if I could hold 60+s or 1:01s for a set of five to ten 100 m fly on the 1:20 send off, then I would feel confident that I could get my second hundred home in 60+ or 1:01. Similarly, I would shoot to hold sets of 50 meters fly on a short rest interval at 30 or preferably faster.

Of course, even if I achieved these practice goals it would not be a guarantee of attaining this goal for Nationals. Nor would this goal provide an exact blueprint for every aspect of training. Nevertheless, it would be one way in which you could use your goals to direct your training, and it would be a check against which each day's swimming could be compared.

Together you and your coach could set similar goals for kicking drills, pulling drills, technique work, weight work, etc. Based on your season or ultimate goals you could set specific training goals that you estimate would be most likely to lead you down the path to success.

Of course, you need to keep your goals flexible. They should be a standard against which you train. But as you improve, you want to readjust your goals. Don't limit yourself with outdated goals.

Act Consistently With Your Goals

When I watch people train or listen to them talk during practices, I often notice that they seem to have the most unlikely goals. Judging from their behavior I speculate that their goals are:

1) To avoid doing anything hard.
2) To go hard only when coach is looking.
3) To get my teammates to go slowly, so I won't look bad.
4) Not to have to lead my lane.
5) To talk coach into longer intervals.
6) To talk coach into fewer repeats.
7) To talk coach into ending practice early.
8) To be the last one in the water at the start of practice.
9) To delay the start of practice by getting coach talking.
10) To see how many extra unseen breaths I can take on a hypoxic series.
11) To see how many laps I can skip without coach noticing.
12) To do less or, better yet, no butterfly.

I doubt any of you would lay claim to these as your chosen goals and aspirations as a swimmer. Yet, how often is your behavior consistent with these type of goals?

Check it out! Stop and take a look at what you are doing in practice. And ask yourself if your behavior is reflective of your goals. If it is not, you need to change your goals to better fit your training behavior or have your behavior more consistently reflect your goals.

Protect Your Goals

Some of the unusual goals mentioned in the previous section seem to become the mode for segments of a team or an entire team. Somehow it becomes "cool" to complain about yardage, to turn around in the middle of a lap without getting caught, to try to get out of doing things at practice, etc. The idea becomes to avoid intense training while going through the motions and circumventing the system.

One of the nice things about swimming is the opportunity to share common goals and a unique lifestyle with people your own age who have similar values. Swimming tends to produce close and lasting friendships. Yet, if your aspirations are high and you act consistently to try to attain them, you sometimes risk straining your friendships.

It's a discouraging dilemma. And, it would be nice if it weren't that way. But the fact remains that some of your friends may not have the drive and dedication you do. Or, they may not share your high goals. Then, your friends may try subtly to coax you into their lazy ways. It's not that they are intentionally trying to drag you down. They just don't want to look bad next to you. So, they invite you to join in their rebellion, confusion, bad habits, or low level of aspiration.

You need not reject your friends, but neither do you have to give up your goals to join the crowd and the fun. If it's hard to do your thing while they are doing theirs, talk to them about it. Don't scold them for their actions, but ask for their acceptance and encouragement in your quest to reach the top.

And encourage your teammates. Pay attention to a job well done by them in practice. Encourage them to strive for more. How you act and what you say to your teammates is contagious and has a way of coming back to you.

Set a norm to get after it; to challenge yourself and others. Don't let the norm become an avoidance of effort. Don't make it "cool" or "in" to goof off.

Remember your goals. And protect them. Take good care of them. You may have to. Others may not have the same goals.

Don't Limit Yourself

Goals can be inspiring. They help you to get absorbed in what you are doing, making your activities more fulfilling. And they supply significant direction. Nevertheless, you should be careful with the form you give to your goals. Precisely because goals do such a good job of directing your efforts, they can limit what you do. That is why I suggest open-ended goals such as: to go at *least* as fast as some specified time.

If you set your goal to break two minutes (and you succeed) you are likely to go a 1:59.9 or thereabouts. Whereas if you set a goal at least to go under two minutes and as far under as you possibly can, you open the door to go a 1:57, a 1:55 or even faster.

Human potential very well may be limitless. Certainly we have not yet discovered its limits, let alone achieved them. It is thinking that we have reached the limits that limits what we do. Believing more is possible opens the doors to unexpected excellence.

You fare much better if you have an open door policy about your goals. Nick Nevid, one of only two swimmers to win a National AAU championship in his first National competition, says, "There's no limit to how fast you can swim." Olympian Bobby Hackett similarly says "...you can never set your goals too high." Attitudes like these direct your activities in a much more desirable and productive direction.

Coach Richard Quick once told me about a descending set of 400 m swims Olympian Tim Shaw swam in preparation for the World Games at Cali. Before the last repeat, Tim was asked what he was going to shoot for on that 400. "Zero!" came the reply as Tim turned and pushed off.

GETTING MOTIVATED

Shoot For Major Breakthroughs In Practice

It is particularly important that you *set open-ended goals for training.* I firmly believe that major breakthroughs occur in practice or at least as a result of the foundation laid in training. That's often hard to see because most often it is at meets, when you are rested, that you swim the fastest. But the breakthroughs that enable you to make major improvements come in training.

It becomes especially important then, that you not limit yourself in practice. Training sessions are the time to shoot for zeroes.

If you strive for a major breakthrough in a meet without the proper preparation, you are likely to go out too fast and/or try too hard. Then in your only chance you'll probably knot up, drag into the finish with the proverbial piano on your back, and end up going slower than if you had hit a pace for which you had trained.

In practice the consequences of attempting a major breakthrough are not the same. If you have never gone a set of ten one hundreds on the minute and you try it and only make three of them before you miss the interval, the worst that happens is you move back over to the 1:05 lane having challenged your body and probably gained some strength and endurance. The next time you try you make make four or five. And soon you'll probably go all ten.

Strive for those zeroes in practice. Unlike meets, practice gives you lots of opportunities for do-overs. And you have nothing to lose.

Make The Most Out Of Each And Every Opportunity

When you train regularly, especially if you train two or three times per day, it is easy to get so lost in the routine that you forget why you are there and what you are trying to accomplish. Often, you are there because it's time for practice. Your thinking may not take it any further than that.

It is difficult to see how one turn, one repeat, one drill or even one whole practice matters that much. The gains are neither that clear nor that immediate.

Furthermore, it is not always the hardest worker who swims the fastest. Especially if you have come up through age group swimming you know that in the younger age groups the bigger, more physically mature, and seemingly more naturally talented athletes often have the greatest success. And, most swimmers improve almost every time out while they are still growing.

Moreover, improvement comes fast and easy at first. A little bit of stroke work, strength building and conditioning brings on major improvements in the novice. As you get older and better and the competition gets tougher, however, improvements are harder earned and come in smaller increments. Then, what you do in practice becomes of greater significance.

Scott Spann insightfully reports this sequence of events:

"I was successful as a young age grouper probably because I was strong for my age and a naturally gifted athlete... I was never known as a worker (to say the least!) even in the primitive swimming methods and work-outs we had."

"By the time I was 13 it began to catch up to me and work became an important factor to success. Swimming was beginning to require what seemed like increased dedication, commitment and discipline..."

13

Yet, even if, like Scott, you come to recognize the importance of consistent intense training, it is still easy to slack off from time to time. And it is difficult to see how that would matter that much. Because, in a sense, it really doesn't. Blow off one repeat, loaf an entire set, or even skip a practice and it is unlikely to matter that much in the long run. It probably will not affect your chances of reaching your goals.

The problem is that you only do one repeat, one set, and one practice at a time. As a result it is difficult to see how that one swim, series or day fits into the scheme of things. It's tremendously difficult to remain constantly aware of the fact that your training is collectively made up of individual repeats, sets and practices. Blowing off one probably won't matter. But that one may be part of a collection that is growing fast and probably will matter very much.

In my clinics for swimmers and in my book *Championship Thinking* I recommend that you think of training as a jar full of unpopped popcorn where each kernel represents one repetition, a practice drill, or a complete day's practice. Your best chance of reaching your goals is to have a full jar of popcorn. But if you remove only one kernel it probably will have no effect on your chances of future success. Certainly, there would be no visibly noticeable difference. And it doesn't really matter which kernel you remove. Remove one. Replace it. Remove another. The jar always appears just as full. Even if you take one out, leave it out, and remove another; it is difficult to notice any difference in the level of the popcorn in the jar; especially from a distance. If you continued to remove kernels from the jar and threw them away, the removal of each one still would be hard to notice. Only as they started to add up, would the difference become clearly noticeable. But then it would be too late. You can't put them back in the jar if you already have thrown them away. If you wanted to reach your goal (a full jar of popcorn), you would hardly choose to throw the whole bunch away at once. But throwing them away one at a time makes it hard to see any effect at all.

So the next time you find yourself faced with a decision to get after a drill or coast through it, to go to practice or to blow it off, or you catch yourself cruising; just say "popcorn" to yourself. You'll know what it means. Then, use that signal to make that opportunity count.

See How The Superstars Train

Most of us find that nothing psyches us up quite so much as watching an exciting major championship. Just being at the Olympics, the World Championships, NCAAs, or Nationals, even as a spectator, is such an electrifying experience that it inspires in most swimmers a determination to get there and win.

Unfortunately, for most swimmers this does little to promote consistent, conscientious training. When it does, the effects are usually short lived.

A more appropriate, but still inspirational experience is to watch someone like Mike Bruner or Tracy Caulkins train. This is more likely to inspire you to emulate the intensity of training that got these swimmers to the top.

Understand Why You Are Doing It

It is difficult to see how each individual training task fits into the entire training program. And, it is even more difficult to understand how what you do today affects how you will perform later this year, especially if the drill differs significantly from what you will be doing when you race.

Why does a sprinter need to do a repeat series of 1000s? Why does a breaststroker need to swim fly? What difference does it make if you go 6500 instead of 7000? And why should anyone strain to do that one extra repetition on the bench press?

Questions like these warrant answers. The better understanding you have of how what you are doing relates to building strength, endurance, flexibility, good stroke mechanics, speed and psychological skills; the more motivated you will be to do it right.

If you don't understand the importance of your training regimen or any part of it, ask your coach to explain it. Now, that doesn't mean you should demand that your coach justify what he or she asks you to do. It means you ask your coach to help you better understand what he or she is trying to help you accomplish, so that that part of training will have more meaning to you and generate greater enthusiasm and motivation to do it right.

Do It Right

Most of us tend to confuse capability with probability. We tend to think that if we have done something correctly once, we

can do it. And since we are capable of doing it, that when it is important we will do it.

It is correct that if you have done something right even once, you surely are capable of doing it. But just because you can, doesn't mean you ever will. When the chips are down, will you do it right, how often and at what cost?

A good example is turns. Once you know how to turn correctly it is easy to assume that you can do it right, if and when you want to. And it is easy to get lazy about turns in practice and to grab a little extra rest, a little extra air, or a little jump on the others around you by gliding in or not stream-lining, by breathing in and out of the turn, or by doing a one-handed turn on fly or breast or turning over on your stomach on backstroke.

You may still be able to do it correctly when it comes to meets. But if you slack off in practice, you have to concentrate more in meets. If you have to think about it, it can slow you down and distract you from your pace. Or, you unthinkingly may do it wrong at the wrong time. After all, if you only do it correctly ten percent of the time in practice, what percentage of the time do you think you will do it right in a meet when you are absorbed in the race and your opponents?

Training is like a labyrinth game. You can find your way through it successfully, but it is difficult. It takes a lot of coordination and concentration. And there are lots of wrong turns and dead end alleys. Even if you have done it before and know the way, it is difficult to react quickly and smoothly enough to keep the ball on track and avoid the pitfalls.

Harder still would be a labyrinth with grooves leading into dead end alleys and sloping toward the pitfalls. You might be able to weave your way around them to make it to the goal. But it would take that much more concentration, coordination, and you would have to travel slower and with greater care. It could be done. But the slightest slip would get the ball caught in the groove, preventing you from reaching your goal.

On the other hand, imagine a labyrinth with a path leading to the goal deeply grooved into the surface. It would enable you to keep the ball rolling smoothly and quickly toward the desired destination despite occasional lapses in concentration.

Habits work similarly. By doing something correctly you groove a path toward your goal. The more often you do it correctly, the deeper you make the groove; making it more likely that that is the way your behavior will flow smoothly and quickly. When you train incorrectly, you groove habits that interfere with good performances.

Think of the labyrinth when you have a choice of turning correctly or being lazy on it, pushing your stroke all the way through or sliding it out, cruising a set or getting after it, or avoiding a practice or drill or eagerly seeking the challenge. Remember, each decision will help groove one kind of habit. Which habits do you want to groove?

18

Ask Keith's Question

Every practice drill matters. Each individual drill combines with every other drill to collectively make up your training. What you do with each drill partly determines your strength, speed, endurance, skill, flexibility, and psychological preparation. Every swim, every turn, every set, every run, every weight repetition helps determine whether you will reach your goals. If in no other way, the way you approach that part of training affects how you approach the rest of training and your races in meets by the way it contributes to forming your habits.

Ideally, you would have a goal for everything you do in training: a goal for each individual drill. That would give each drill some meaning and purpose, get you absorbed in what you are doing, keep you building toward your long term goals and help keep you motivated to do it right. Of course, if you swim for a team you do not design your own training program. In fact, you probably do not even know what the next drill will be until immediately before you are to start on it. You can, however, identify a goal to be accomplished in the few seconds in between when you learn what you are to do next and the start of the series.

Once you know what you are to do, ask yourself Keith's Question. Then, convert the answer to action.

KEITH'S QUESTION: "What can I do to get the most out of this set and have fun while doing it?"

It is important to convert your answer to Keith's Question to action. It isn't enough to identify a way of deriving the most benefit out of a set and a way to enjoy that quest for improvement. You might know what you want to do, without doing it! That would serve you little purpose. To gain the benefits from asking Keith's Question, *you must do it! You must take the specified action!*

STAYING MOTIVATED

Think in terms of "Want To's," not "Have To's"

If you think you "have to" do something, you tend to resist it. No one wants to be forced to do anything. If you decide you "want to" do something there's probably no stopping you.

Think of your training in terms of "want to's". If you have made your training meaningful, understand how it relates to your goals and keep your eye on your goals, a "Do I have to swim this set?" a "Do I have to go fly?" or even an "I don't want to go a 2000," easily can become an *I want to!*

Actively Remind Yourself What You Are Accomplishing

From time to time you may find yourself asking "Why am I doing this?" You may question the utility of a certain drill or the importance of swimming at all. Or you may confuse yourself with an "I don't want to do this" (with an eye to your immediate wants, without consideration to your long term objectives).

When the going gets tough, it is important that you talk sense to yourself. Remind yourself of how the training you are doing will contribute to success. And seek to maintain an appropriate balance between your immediate wants and your future aspirations.

Tell yourself things like:

"I'm building strength."

"This may be boring, but it is building endurance."

"Stay after it. You want to make the interval and you want to groove good habits."

"Feeling more comfortable now is not as important as stressing my body and building strength."

"Popcorn."

Keep An Eye On Your Goals

Remind yourself of where you are going and what you want to achieve. Your goals can provide a lot of incentive if you keep them close at hand. Keep an eye on your goals.

Montreal Olympian Bruce Furniss says that "Ever since my brother brought home a bronze medal in 1972, from that day on I've thought about the Olympic Games."

Flyer Camille Wright reported that "When I get bored at workout,...I think of the Nationals for motivation. I want to be up there—No. 1. I think of that a lot when I'm doing my fly repeats. I want to be within range of my best time."

Like Camille it is important that you use your goals as incentives to inspire action. Fantasizing about Nationals, the Olympics or a World Record is just that: fantasy. Use your goals to inspire you to *do* the training that will get you there.

Make Intense Training Fun

Earlier I said training is designed as a means to an end. But with the volume of training being what it is these days it has become more than that. To a swimmer, training is not only preparation for meets, it is a lifestyle.

If your life is going to center largely around your swimming, you might as well make intense training fun and enjoy your lifestyle. It isn't that hard to do.

The main difference between work and play is how you view it. If you think of your training as fun and look for the challenge and exhilaration in what you do, practices can be an enjoyable part of the day, one you look forward to. If you view training as a necessary evil and label your work-outs as boring, tedious, and painful, you are likely to look forward only to getting out early or skipping practice altogether.

Don't bring yourself down by thinking about the things you do not like about practice. If you want to, you can always find some of those to complain about, to worry about, and to feel sorry for yourself about. But you might just as easily decide you like these very same things. And it is much more fun, and a lot more useful, to focus on the things you do like. Pay more attention to the fun parts of swimming!

SWIMMING IS FUN! Don't make it a drag by thinking it's not!

Make A Game Out Of It

Olympic Freestyle Champion Mike Burton once said "I'm not really sure what the right kind of attitude is. But I know one thing, you can't mind a lot of work... I like to win each repeat. You have to swim with each one real hard. You get into the habit of winning. This keeps me working, I sort of make a game out of it."

Olympic Butterfly Champion Mike Bruner similarly sought out the challenge and made games of training drills. He would push off on his turns, streamline, kick and see how long he could keep up with another swimmer without starting his stroke. He tried to find another swimmer approaching the wall (no matter if the other swimmer had 2 laps to go) and tried to beat him to the finish, simulating a touch out situation.

With some creativity you can make a game out of every drill. And by doing so you can get more engaged in practice, more motivated, and make intense training more fun.

Appreciate Taking Your Body To The Limit

The practices that I enjoy the least are the ones where I go through the motions. The ones I enjoy the most are the ones I really get after.

It just plain feels good to be swimming, loose, fast, and taking your body to the limits. That is a large part of what makes racing fun. And probably what got you into swimming in the first place.

Granted there is fatigue to deal with. And often the difficult part is getting going in the first place, not keeping it up. But reminding yourself how exhilarating it is to stretch yourself to the limits and how satisfying it is to have done so, will help you get after it.

Once you do, appreciate it. There is really nothing like it. It is an exciting and rewarding phenomenon that only a few select individuals ever get to experience. Others never get in good enough shape to make the trip.

Pat Yourself On The Back

Part of the problem in staying motivated to train is that the payoffs are so far down the road and often very uncertain. That is one reason it is so important to set goals for training. The satisfaction of reaching these goals goes a long way toward maintaining your interest.

Don't be afraid to pat yourself on the back for a job well done (even if you only did what you were "supposed" to do). Don't make light of your daily accomplishments. Each drill can be a tremendous challenge. Accepting that challenge and meeting it head on should be applauded.

Make a point of telling yourself how well you did and congratulating yourself for it. Emphasize the things you did do well. Be proud of the intervals you made, the times you held on repeats, and the effort you put out.

When you slip and do less well than you thought you could, use this temporary setback to give you new direction. But don't dwell on it. Accentuate the positive. The more weight you give to your good performance and the more often you reward yourself for a job well done, the more often you will get after it in practice.

Once in a while make a point of treating yourself to a movie, a t-shirt, record album or some other treat as a reward for an especially good practice. If you reach your goals, that probably will be reward enough. But rewarding yourself along the way only serves to make it easier to get there and makes the trip more fun.

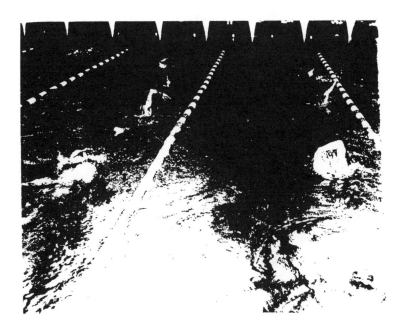

TRAINING EFFICIENTLY

Use The Clock

The pace clock is an invaluable tool for training. Make the most of it.

It is difficult to stay focused on what you are trying to accomplish when practices last for a couple of hours and take place in a static and barren environment. Your attention is bound to wander. Frequent use of KEITH'S QUESTION helps. So does keeping an eye on the pace clock with your mind's eye on your goals.

The clock helps you compare your practice performances with your training goals. It lets you know if your efforts are on target. It leaves little doubt.

From time to time, too many of us tend to get casual about our use of the clock. We tend instead to rely on our internal reading of the amount of effort exerted as a way of judging whether we are descending a set or generally training hard. In addition to the inaccuracy of such a measure, there are other problems with relying on effort to guide your training.

There is such a thing as trying too hard. The goal is to swim as fast as possible. That necessitates intense effort. But you do not necessarily go faster the harder you try. Pace and efficiency count.

Train by the clock. Learn how it feels to swim fast, not necessarily hard! If you go faster with less effort than you do with more, all the better. You'll just be able to maintain that faster pace longer.

And it doesn't mean you're not working. Consistently getting after it is commendable, but not necessarily more noble than swimming fast with less effort. Most likely if you are swimming fast with less effort, you are swimming more efficiently and have more room to improve by exerting more effort at that same level of efficiency without over-trying.

So, guide and judge your training performance by the clock, not by how it feels. Feel can be deceptive. The clock never lies.

Relax: Swim Loose, But Fast

Have you ever had the experience where you were having one of those days (or sets) where you just didn't seem to have it? You just couldn't get going. You were trying, but it just wasn't there to be found. Then something happened. Your coach came over and stood over you, closely watching your swim. Or you decided to bust the last repeat of a series. Or someone, who you hate to have beat you, started to pass you. Or maybe you got angry at someone in your lane. Whatever brought it out, all of a sudden you seemed to break through the sluggishness that seemed to be holding you back. From then on, you were able to attack your practice like you wouldn't have thought possible a moment before.

Often that sluggishness comes from not wanting to be there, having doubts about your ability or present condition, or worry of one form or another. One result of this kind of psychological activity is an increase in muscle tension that interferes with your efforts to get after it. This over abundance of muscle tension gets you pitting one muscle against another. Then, when something happens to divert your attention away from your tension-producing doubts or worry, you relax and pick it up.

This differential relaxation (relaxing unneeded muscle groups, while appropriately tensing the muscles you need to swim) is a key to efficient, fast, smooth, powerful performances. Practice it while you swim. Stay as relaxed as you possibly can in your face and other muscles you are not using. And attend carefully to relaxing muscles antagonistic to the prime movers. Relax and swim loose, but fast.

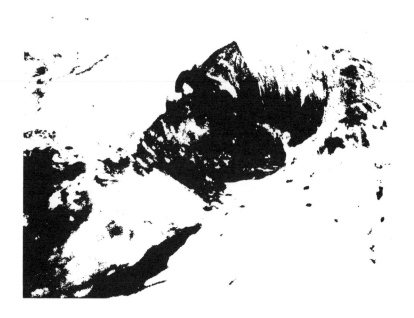

MANAGING DISCOMFORT

Welcome The Pain Of Training Hard

If you are to build strength, speed and endurance, you have to stress your muscles and your body's capacity to produce energy. This necessitates extending yourself beyond the limits of physical and psychological comfort.

Handling this discomfort, or the "pain" produced in swimming, can be one of, if not, the most formidable challenges facing you in your quest for excellence. Nobody likes to hurt. And the challenge is made even tougher because the hurt doesn't just happen. It is self-inflicted. You have to hurt yourself to improve.

If you see "having to" "hurt" as something bad and the "pain" as "bad" or even "awful" or "intolerable," you make it more difficult to make the decision to get after your training and to stay with it when you do.

Don't view the sensations that accompany an effortful swim as bad. Welcome them. See them as natural physiological signs that you are working hard, building strength, gaining stamina, and going fast.

View pain as a positive sign, a signal of growth and a sign that you are making progress. Then pushing yourself to the limits can be something you actively seek out instead of something you shy away from.

Handle The Pain In The Present

The pain involved in swimming is not that bad. It can be discomforting, but never intolerable. What often is most difficult to handle is the anticipation that it is coming or the subtle fear that it will get worse and you won't be able to handle it. Doc Counsilman even has been quoted as saying that "The goal of training is to get swimmers to stop fearing pain."

There is no question fatigue is a real detriment to performance. But most swimmers lose it psychologically before they do physically. Don't let that be your usual reaction. Stay with the present. You can handle whatever pain accompanies that stroke or even the lap you are on. It's not that bad. Remind yourself of that fact. And don't worry about what's to come. Remind yourself that when it comes you can handle it. Anticipation is the worst part.

Use The Pain As A Signal To Pick It Up

As you push yourself in practice, stress your muscles, and go into oxygen debt, you often begin to notice the pain of effort and fatigue. The natural response is to back off. But you do not have to do that. In fact, it is important that you do not ease up. Here is where you get the most out of your training. Moreover, feeling tired or hurting does not have to be a signal to slow down.

Use the pain as a signal to pick it up. NCAA Freestyle Champion Jack Tingley used pain in this fashion. He was once quoted as saying "When I get a pain, I try to go harder and swim faster. That way, I really don't get rid of the pain, but at least I tend to forget it's there since I'm concentrating on something else."

Former American Record holder Lee Engstrand feels it is important to stay with it when you are hurting. "I feel that when a swimmer gets tired and starts hurting, the more he can do after that, the better off he will be. You learn more when you start hurting. I back off sometimes, but when I do, I feel that I have cheated myself out of something."

Don't cheat yourself. Use the pain as a signal to stay with it and pick it up. Give it all you've got, then pick it up. Do all you think you can. Then, go some more. Build the kind of habits you want to show up in a race. And use practice swims to develop the strength and stamina it's going to take in meets to use the pain as a signal to pick it up.

Use The Pain As A Signal To Relax

If you are afraid of the pain or worry about its effects or your ability to handle it, you tighten up. That increased muscular tension exaggerates the feel of the pain. It interferes with the rapid, strong and fluid use of your muscles. And it needlessly wastes energy, tiring you out even more.

Use the pain as a signal to relax, stay loose, and stretch it out. You really do get tired. There's no use in making it worse.

Decide There Is No Pain In Swimming

One of the best ways of *accepting the pain* as a natural physical response to effort and eliminating dreading it is to not think of it in the same way you think of other "pains" and "hurts." Don't even call it pain. Think of these sensations as signals of a build up of lactic acid, oxygen debt, or partial muscle fatigue.

Lothar Kipke, the G.D.R. national team physician, once told me: "There is no pain in swimming. Pain is when they (swimmers) are sick or injured. Pain is bad. Sports are fun. They never go together." You too can decide there is no pain in swimming.

BUILDING CONFIDENCE

Lay A Solid Foundation For Confidence

Now is the time to lay a solid foundation for the confidence you will want when it comes time for the meet. You know that you build strength, speed, flexibility, good stroke technique, endurance and good psychological habits through rigorous, conscientious training and practice. You can't be confident without doing the training. Conversely, there is no surer way to feel confident come meet time, than to have put in the practice.

After his first National Championship victory in 1978 in the 100 m freestyle David McCagg spoke about believing in himself and feeling confident as a result of his training:

"Before I was never really mentally prepared. But at this meet I felt a little more relaxed and prepared for the race... We do a lot of land exercise and wheels and I believe in them. They really build you up. I believe strength is where it's at. The important thing is just believing in myself, believing in my training and the fact that I can win."

Camille Wright echoed the fact that laying a foundation in training yielded confidence for her at meets:

"The more fly repeats I do in training, the better I think I'll do." Do it now. Then later you will know it is there!

Believe In Yourself

David McCagg attributed his success largely to his confidence in his training program, and his "believing in myself... and the fact that I can win." Olympic Champion Brian Goodell similarly professes a strong belief in himself when he reports "I've set goals for myself that you might think are unrealistic, but

I know I can achieve them. Whether it's a certain time for a specific set or the level of intensity with which I do the swim, I'm going all out this season like never before."

Notice how integrally tied their expressed belief in themselves is to their efforts and their training. Confidence is always based on action. The more you've done in training and the more success you've had in meets, the easier it is to believe in yourself. But a belief in yourself must be based on a solid foundation and the expectation that you will do what it takes to meet the challenge.

Without this commitment to action, a belief in yourself is an illusion, an overconfidence based on fantasy. If overconfident, you don't think it matters what you do. You think you will win anyway. That is as much of a problem as not believing in yourself, where you think it doesn't matter what you do because you think you will lose anyway.

A belief in yourself reflects the expectation that *with a concerted effort* you will succeed, and the commitment to put forth that effort. Make that commitment. Give yourself a reason to believe.

Remove The Word "Can't" From Your Vocabulary

If you think about it, it really ought to be easy to believe in yourself. There is never any conclusive evidence that you can't do something. Certainly there never is any conclusive evidence that you can't swim faster.

Maybe you have never won a race. Perhaps you've never made a set of hundreds on a certain interval. Maybe you have never swum a 200 fly before without breaking your stroke. But none of these need be any indication of what you will do the next time out. They really aren't even any indication of what you were capable of in the past. They don't necessarily mean you can't or even that you couldn't. They only mean you did not.

No one has ever posted a sub-2 minute 200 m breaststroke or a sub-40 second 100 yard free. That doesn't mean it can't be done. It doesn't even mean it won't be done. Nor, does it mean that *you* won't do it. It just hasn't happened yet.

"Can't" is not correct. We don't have any definitive way of placing a ceiling on human potential. Moreover, everyday we are doing things that used to be deemed impossible.

Beyond not being correct, the word "can't" is not useful. Even if you don't really mean it, but mean something like "I'm having difficulty," "I haven't recently," "I haven't yet," or "I won't;" the sentiment has a way of limiting your motivation, your confidence and your actions. Somehow saying "I can't" seems to make it so.

MENTAL REHEARSAL

Groove-In Super Swims

Everyone thinks and daydreams about winning swimming. Put some planning to this process and better use it to your advantage.

Use your imagination to practice swimming the way you want to swim. Notice I suggest practicing *swimming* the way you want to swim, not merely visualizing the desired results.

Picturing the results can be inspiring. If that spurs you to action and encourages confidence, it is extremely valuable. Moreover, picturing yourself as a winner helps get you more comfortable with the prospect of victory and all it entails. Don't neglect, however, the swim necessary to get you there.

Regularly visualize your goal-swim with great attention to detail. Picture it vividly. Feel the water as you flow across it. Feel your muscles powerfully speed you to your destination. See what you will see when you are absorbed in the race. Hear the muffled noise of the crowd, the sizzling of the air bubbles, and the gentle slapping of your stroke against the water. Smell the odor of the chlorine. Experience how it feels to swim fast. Talk to yourself the way you will want to in the race.

Olympic champion and the first man under 50 seconds for the 100 m freestyle, Jim Montgomery emphasizes the importance of realistic, vivid, detailed imagery. He suggests "Every swimmer visualizes his race. It's getting the details of the race that is important."

Regularly practice your swims imaginally. When combined with physical training, mental rehearsal will groove-in super swims.

Rehearse The Entire Meet Experience

Most swimmers visualize their races. You should too. But don't limit your mental rehearsal of meets to the physical side of the race. Imaginally practice all that goes into making a successful meet performance.

Practice handling the pressure. Imagine yourself coping with your worries by relaxing, keeping things in perspective and focusing on the race instead of the outcome.

Visualize yourself feeling confident. Imaginally practice thinking confidently, feeling at home, and acting confident.

Steve Lundquist, the first man under two minutes for a 200 yd. breaststroke, reportedly programs his belief in himself nearly every night by listening to a record that suggests:

"You can be the best in the world. You can set world records... You were born to be a winner...

TRIUMPH! TRIUMPH! TRIUMPH! TRIUMPH!"

Rehearse where you want your head to be during the race. Practice forceful self-talk to guide you through the tough parts. Repeatedly practice making the choice to seize every opportunity and milk it for all it's worth.

Psychology is a critical part of performance. Use your imagination to practice for good psychological performance as well as good physical execution.

Build Good Training Habits

Your mental rehearsal of meets should not be limited to the race itself. Nor should you limit your imaginal practice to rehearsing the competitive experience. Groove-in good training habits by using your imagination to practice meeting the challenges of training.

Mental practice is a poor substitute for physical training. It doesn't build strength and stamina. But it does make for good psychological habits. And when combined with physical practice it reinforces stroke technique and race strategy.

Use your imagination to make a high level of self-motivation for training a habit. Visualize yourself making the most out of practices. Picture yourself catching yourself slacking off and turning it around.

Groove-in a habit of enjoying training. Imaginally practice eagerly attacking every drill.

Mentally rehearse coping with the "partial muscle fatigue" that challenges consistent rigorous training. And run a movie through your mind of you confidently approaching each training drill without limiting yourself.

Good habits are formed with practice. Add to your opportunities to practice by using your imagination.

THE BOTTOM LINE

Do It Now

Putting things off for later is not a way of delaying them. It is a way of never getting them done; at least in training for competitive swimming.

In training you can't make up for what you miss. Each day, each practice, each drill, each swim only comes once. Once you let that opportunity pass, it is gone forever. You can make good use of your next swim, series or practice; but you cannot recapture the opportunity you missed. From the entire popcorn jar of training, you threw away one kernel.

You can't put off going to practice until tomorrow. You can't put off challenging yourself on a repeat until later. Later never comes for that practice or that repeat. Later is a misnomer given to a future and different now.

Take advantage of each chance. This is your only opportunity to get anything out of today. Use it. Do it now!

It's Up To You

There's an old adage (that I just made up) that says "you can lead a swimmer to a good training program, but you can't make him train right." Your coach can produce a program designed to elicit championship performances. Your team can provide the facilities and equipment you need. Your parents, coach, teammates and friends can provide you with support and encouragement. But *you* have to get the job done.

Take responsibility for what you get out of training. Take responsibility for what you do. It's up to you to form good habits. It's up to you to make intense training fun. You are responsible for your moods, your feelings, and your behavior (even your unthinking acts).

No matter how much others may wish to help you, what you put into your training and what you get out of it is *ultimately up to you!* No one can do it for you.

MEETS

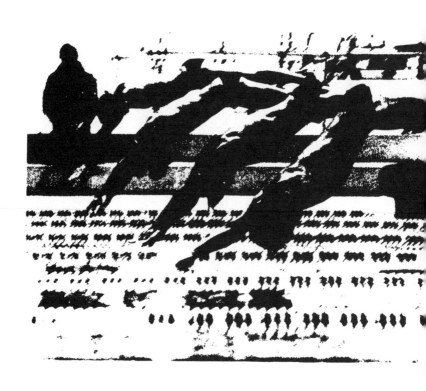

THE SUPER PSYCH

For all the benefits to be derived from training (and I think they are considerable), the main purpose of training is to prepare for the meets. Meets are where you put it all on the line. And meets are where the payoff for all your training is there for the taking.

Sometimes you put it all together and swim out of your mind. When you do, there is nothing like it. Those magic moments when you are really "smoking" not only put you in the running, but feel so good. They are the swimmer's ultimate high.

But those super swims seem elusive and fragile. They seem to come only with a well-planned and executed training regimen, a healthy body, a shave, just the right taper, a well-designed and executed race plan and a super psych.

Good psychology is critical! It looms especially important now when everyone is training hard and success is determined by tenths, hundreths, thousandths and sometimes even ten-thousandths of a second. But good psychology need not be elusive. You can learn to apply good psychology to help you produce peak swims more consistently.

Let me show you how.

GETTING UP FOR MEETS

Strive To Get "Up" For Every Meet

Most of the time getting up for the meets is no problem. Meets are what you train for. The payoffs are there. And racing is fun. It is exciting, challenging and exhilarating.

Sometimes, however, you may have trouble getting psyched for a meet. You may not care if you win. You may expect to win easily. You may expect to do poorly. You may be afraid of losing, or of hurting. Or, some combination of these factors may act to inhibit motivation.

No matter why you find it difficult to get psyched, you've still got to get up for the meet. Every meet counts.

You've Got To Care

Many swimmers tell me they feel it is important that they get nervous before a race. If they are not nervous, they don't seem to do as well. They get too casual about their races.

The important thing is not that you are nervous but that you care. It just happens that when you care, you tend to get nervous.

You've got to care. If you don't care about your races, you are likely to approach them too casually. You probably will fail to concentrate enough. You probably will fail to give it all you've got. You even may not try at all.

If you care, if you really want it, you won't hold anything back. You will give your all.

Provide Yourself With Some Incentive

Some of the less important meets may seem to lack excitement and rewards. Some meets may not mean that much to you.

This seems to be partially a hazard of experience. Early in your swimming career, every meet is exciting and a challenge. The trophies, medals and even ribbons hold great appeal. But with experience the novelty wears off, some of the rewards disappear, and other rewards diminish in importance.

For some people it is hard to care about another medal when you've got boxes full in your closet. If you have competed for National Titles, a place on the Olympic Team, or National Team trips, a local meet may fail to inspire you. And as you get better, improvements come in smaller increments, are harder earned and occur less often. Then, you may think you need a shave, a taper and top competition in order to swim your best. As a result, many meets fail to seem special. They just seem like another meet. Then, it's tough to get "up" for it.

But there is always something there for you—if you look. Find it and provide yourself with some incentive. Remind yourself of the challenge of competing, if even only against yourself. Think of the exhilaration waiting for you when completely engaged in striving to do the best you can do, here, today, and under these conditions.

Look at each race as an opportunity to reach a goal you have for yourself. If you don't have one, set one. It doesn't have to be your ultimate goal. It can be one step up the ladder to the ultimate.

View your race as a chance for a personal record. And remind yourself of team goals for the meet and how you can contribute.

If nothing else, provide yourself with some incentive by reminding yourself that even if the outcome doesn't seem that important, the habits you build are. Lesser meets are your best opportunities to practice for the big meets.

Overcome Complacency

At some meets you may expect victory to come easy. There may be no competition for you. But don't let overconfidence impede motivation and concentration. You may fail to try, if you think you will win no matter what.

Attack this kind of complacency with reminders of the importance of doing well. Remind yourself that meets provide great opportunity to practice for races that probably will be more tightly contested. Remind yourself of the habits you want to groove.

And remind yourself that winning may not be as easy as it seems. If you go all out, victory may come easily. But a lackadaisical swim might cause the win to slip away.

Swim The Best Race You Can, Here, Now And Under These Conditions

Sometimes, you lack confidence and expect to do poorly. Maybe you are swimming through the meet and are tired. Maybe you think other swimmers have got you outclassed because you are swimming an off event or you just think you are out of your league. But you needn't let any of that hamper your motivation.

Every race finds you with whatever shape, strength, and skill that you have at that time. Whatever that is, that is where you are at the moment. It is too late to change that for this meet. But you can swim the best race you can, here, now, and under these conditions. Remind youself of that fact. And give it all you've got.

HANDLING THE PRESSURE

Don't Make Your Races Too Precious

Meets are fun. Keep them that way. Don't make them scary by worrying about hurting, making it or about the ill effects of losing. Meets can't be fun if you are afraid.

You've got to care. But don't make the results of your races too precious. If you do, it seems like you "have to" do well. The prospect of not winning or of doing poorly seems awful. As a result, you can get too tense to do well. Or, you may even feign not caring because you are afraid to lose. Heck, if you don't try, you can't fail, right?... Wrong! If you don't try, you're sure to fail!

Don't swim to avoid doing poorly or to not lose. Swim to go fast. Strive to win.

Stay Focused On Your Real Goals

Sometimes you get nervous or complacent by verbalizing relatively foolish goals. For example, I've often heard swimmers reply to a question about what they are shooting for on a 200 fly, 400 I.M. or 1500 free with such ambitious goals as "to make it" or "to finish."

Obviously if you thought about it in light of the amount of training you have put in, you wouldn't really doubt your ability to make it. But talking about it, even kiddingly, can raise some doubts and get you nervous.

Granted you don't really mean it when you report such goals. Instead, such comments usually are designed to be psych-out tactics or to take the pressure off by altering others' expectations. The problem is they sometimes subtly act to alter *your* expectations and motivations. Talking about trying to "make it" obscures your real goals. Then, you may find yourself approaching your race as casually as you might if you really were just trying to make it, rather than bringing to bear the intensity and concentration your real goals warrant.

Stay focused on your real goals. Leave the cute talk and verbal games to others.

Don't Put Your Ego On The Line

Most of the anxiety stemming from the prospect of not doing well comes from equating yourself with your performance. The fear comes from viewing swimming as if how well you swim somehow determines how good a person you are.

If you think of yourself as a failure, if you fail to reach your goals and if you think of yourself as no good, if you swim poorly; then you tend to be afraid of failing or doing poorly. You strive to avoid losing, instead of seeking to win. Before the race you tend to worry about how well you will do instead of relaxing and planning how you want to swim. During the race you tend to focus on how well you are doing, instead of paying attention to what you are doing.

Contest the race, not yourself. Don't put your ego on the line with each race. Vie for medals, trophies, world records, championships, best times, trips, etc.; not for a good feeling about yourself. How well you do is not an accurate measure of how good you are. You are not what you swim. Thinking you are only increases the pressure.

It's not okay to fail. You want to enthusiastically strive for excellence and pursue each win. But you are okay, even if you fail. There's a big difference!

Strive For Perfection, But Don't Demand You Swim The Perfect Race

Usually you train and prepare all season long for one or two big meets. When it comes, you shave, taper and make sure you are eating and sleeping right. You work to get the right psychological state and the best race plan. You strain to get every ounce of capability out to meet this challenge. You want to put it all together at this time. You strive to make this one race the perfect one.

There is nothing wrong with striving for perfection. And certainly the big meet is the time to do it. These opportunities are few and far between. But often, because it is so important, you put too much pressure on yourself to do it right; to swim the perfect race.

Strive for perfection, but don't demand it. Nobody ever swims the perfect race. There is always room for improvement.

Get excited about the chance and go after it. That will get you to eagerly seek the challenge. Demanding perfection, on the other hand, only gets you avoiding imperfection, feeling the pressure, and trying too hard.

Add A "So" To Your "What Ifs"

A little nervousness is natural. But you don't want to let it get out of hand. If it becomes noticeably disturbing, attack it at its source, before it takes its toll.

One source of nervousness is the "What ifs": "What if I don't make cuts?" "What if I go out too slow?" "What if I go out too fast?" "What if I don't make the team?" etc. The "What ifs" are rarely answered, but the implication is that it would be terrible.

Get specific about what would be terrible about falling short of your goals. Ask yourself: "What is the worst that can happen?" Getting specific about your fears tends to defuse them.

Add a "So" to your "What ifs." Ask yourself "So what if _____?" Take the worst that can happen and see if it is really that bad. That will give you a more realistic perspective and help put you at ease.

Keep Your Races In Perspective

You strive to do the very best you can possibly do. You train long and hard to prepare for the opportunity to compete. And you want to win. Clearly the object of the sport of competitive swimming is to swim faster than anyone else. Those who swim the fastest reap the rewards. But how bad is it really, if you do not do as well as you would like to or even as well as you think you are capable of at that moment?

True, the number of meets, especially the big ones, is limited. Naturally, it would be disappointing to let those opportunities slip by. But missing a chance to get something good is not the same as getting something bad.

Keep your races in the proper perspective. Don't let the threat of possible disappointment quell your eagerness to swim and get you so tight that you insure what you fear.

A poor swim is not the end of the world. Especially if you made a point of enjoying your training, this one race need not be that precious. You have nothing to lose except the opportunity. But you have a lot to gain!

Save Your Energy For The Race

Before a race, relax. Nervousness and worry waste energy. Anxiety tightens and fatigues your muscles. And it burns energy.

After his 1976 Olympic 100 m breaststroke victory John Hencken thoughtfully observed: "I was very relaxed and you swim better when you're relaxed."

Relaxation reduces oxygen consumption, loosens and rests your muscles. Conserve your energy. Relax! Save it for the race.

Take Your Mind Off The Race

If you can't think about the upcoming race without getting nervous, don't think about it. Take your mind off the race by getting involved in some relaxing activity instead.

The Soviet National Team psychologist prepares a book of jokes and anecdotes for each swimmer and gives it to them to read at big meets. I find it helps me relax if I tell jokes to the timers right before I swim.

You might like to get lost in some good music, travel somewhere peaceful in your head, or play cards. Whatever works to keep you relaxed and unconcerned (unconcerned, not uncaring!) about your race, do it.

Ideally, you have put in the training, planned and rehearsed your race in advance. Now is not the time to do too much preparation or to worry. Now is the time to relax and enjoy the meet.

Focus On The Swim, Not The Results

If you do think about your upcoming race while waiting, make sure your thoughts focus on the swim, not on the results. Focusing on the swim allows you to prepare for the race by implanting some last minute instructions to think about during your swim. Thinking of the results may invite the "What ifs" and only get you nervous. In any case, you can do something about how you swim. You can't do anything about the results, except by controlling your swim.

Camille Wright says that before a race her coach would tell her a few things to concentrate on during the race:

> "He'll tell me... Little things like, 'On the first four strokes, don't push it. Just find your stroke.' That's so I won't spin the water. Then he'll tell me to stretch out of the turn and put my head down... And finally, he'll tell me the most important thing is to finish... The last 10 meters are the most important of the whole race... So when I dive in I'm thinking, 'four strokes, stretch on the turn, and finish.' ... Then I don't think about other things, like who's over there in lane 1."

NCAA backstroke champion Clay Britt says that before his races he always goes through the race in his head. He wants to identify one or two key points to focus on during his swim because "Sometimes you get a mental lapse during the race. That's what I'm trying to overcome. Getting that one point to think about helps."

If you do think about your upcoming race while waiting to swim, use this time to plan. Like Clay and Camille, focus on the swim, not the results.

Some Nervousness Is Natural, But Put It To Work For You

As long as you want to do well, you are likely to experience at least a little nervousness before a race. It can tighten you up a little and waste some energy. But don't worry about it draining you. That would only increase your nervousness. You're in good enough shape that a little nervousness won't hurt.

Accept some nervousness as natural. It need not be bad. In fact it can help.

Olympic Champion Bruce Furniss reveals, "There's no question I get highly emotional. When it means something to you and you've worked very hard and put out a lot, naturally you're going to be a little nervous."

"The thing that I've learned to do is channel that emotion to work for me instead of against me. Instead of getting all tight and scared and upset, I just say, 'It's a good sign. I'm ready and I'll do well.'"

Interpret the nervousness as a sign that you care. Then, put it to work for you. Use it as a signal to stay relaxed until the race. Then use it as a spur to intense, concentrated, explosive action!

POSITIVE SWIMMING

Never Doubt What You're Not Sure About

Mike Bruner once suggested "You have to feel...that you have the capabilities to win it." It's true. Without that expectation, you are liable to resign yourself to defeat and not even try. If you really believe you can win, that confidence helps you find ways to produce victory.

It should be easy to believe in yourself. You never have any reason to doubt your ability. You never have any evidence that you can't do something. You may know you never did it before, but that hardly means you cannot do it now or sometime in the future.

One nice thing about swimming is that the outcome of a race is never certain until it is over. No matter how many big names are entered, they still have to do it in the water. And

some unknown can always make a big drop and scoop up a National Championship like Nick Nevid did in his first Nationals. Who knows? You might do it too.

Help yourself by believing in your capabilities. Never doubt something you're not sure about.

Dwell On The Positive

Get in the habit of believing in yourself by dwelling on the positive. Think of the things you do well and your capabilities. Affirm your general tendencies to take positive action.

Think affirmations like "I enjoy a challenge," "I train diligently," "I like to give that little extra," "I make the most out of my training," "I can do it," "I swim well when the pressure is on." This kind of thinking fosters a general confidence and opens the door to consistent excellence.

Think You Will Do It

Affirmations boost confidence. But knowing you are capable of swimming fast is not enough. You must also believe you *will* swim fast.

Think of exactly what you *will do* to bring your capabilities to bear in pursuit of your goals. Tell yourself things like, "I'm going to get out in the lead and build it," "I'm going to get out loose and fast and negative split it," "I'm going to hold off every challenge."

Predict success with great certainly. Emphasize that you *will do* what it takes to succeed. Stress the action, not the results.

Thinking you will do it helps elicit confidence. But, of course, the magic in this kind of thinking only works when it is accompanied by action.

If you tell yourself you are "going to get out in the lead and build it" and you take the lead, it becomes easier to confidently think you are going to build your lead and to confidently go about doing so. Start a chain reaction where confidence yields successful action and successful action builds more confidence.

Remind Yourself Of The Foundation You've Laid

It is much easier to view your races with confidence if you know you are prepared. Consistent, intense training lays a solid foundation for confidence.

As you approach your races remind yourself of all the things you did to prepare. Even if you haven't trained perfectly (no one ever does), now is not the time to dwell on any imperfections. Remind yourself of the distance you did put in; the times you did get after it; and the strength, stamina and flexibility you did build. Accentuate the positive. (Of course, the better you have trained, the more you have to remind yourself of.)

Brian Goodell used this strategy to feel confident at the 1976 Olympic Trials. There, for the first time, he knew he was able to win. He says, "I just knew that I was much better this year than I had ever been before, because I worked so much harder."

Replay Past Successes

Remind yourself of past successes. Success yields success. Jack Tingley once commented, "Every time I go faster, it helps my confidence. I have the feeling that I know I can win and that helps." You too can experience confidence by re-experiencing past successes.

Generate confidence by replaying your good swims in your mind. Even better, if available, view your past successes on film. NCAA backstroke champion, Clay Britt regularly views films of his races. His main purpose in doing so is to critically examine the technical side of his race, but Clay says it "helps confidence to see yourself swim well." "I get a good feeling knowing that I can do it again," he says. He goes on to say that "You get the feeling you had then. And if you carry it into your next race, you can do better."

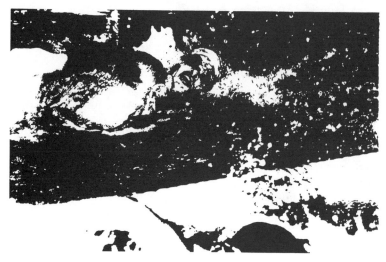

Preplay Success

Nothing generates confidence like knowing you have already successfully done something before. If you haven't done it yet, preplay success.

Not many swimmers have experienced breaking a world record, winning the Olympics, making the Olympic team, etc. Yet having already achieved these goals makes it easier to be confident of attaining them again. Insure confidence by reaching these heights in practice.

If you can break the World Record in practice, it will make it that much easier to do it in a meet. If nothing else, you can always do it in advance imaginally.

Experience what it is like to produce that winning performance. And learn what it is like to have won. Make winning a reality. Something you know well.

Know What To Expect

It's hard to feel confident when you have any uncertainty at all. Don't let unfamiliarity and uncertainty about the facility, the procedures or the atmosphere flow over into a general feeling of uncertainty that invades your approach to your race.

Get to know the pool, the procedures, and the routine. If possible swim in a prior meet at the same pool. If you can't arrange that, try to visit the pool in advance. At least get there early enough to give yourself a chance to get acclimated.

Get to know what to expect. If you've never been to Nationals before, ask someone what it is like. Get pictures of the pool or, at least, a description. Ask others what it feels like to compete at this level. Visualize what it will be like to be there during the meet. Be prepared.

Act Confident

Act confident and appear confident. Even if you do not feel confident, act as if you do. Just acting as if you are confident will generate a genuine confidence.

Radiate confidence. Looking confident will get others to help you build on these feelings by the way they respond to you.

Relax. Stay calm, collected and self-assured. Sit or stand up straight and tall, but relaxed and comfortable.

Avoid staring at your competition. Let other swimmers watch you.

Strut your stuff. Carry yourself like a winner. You'll feel like one. And others will assume you are one.

A POSITIVE MEET PSYCHOLOGY

Don't Be Afraid To Hurt. It's Never That Bad

It is amazing how you can train 6,000 to 20,000 meters a day and then approach a race with some fear of hurting. The truth is, if you have put in the training and you concentrate on swimming as fast as you possibly can, you probably won't notice much discomfort in a race. You will be too focused on trying to go fast. Certainly, if you have been practicing dealing with it in training by welcoming it as a sign of growth, relaxing, staying in the present and dealing with only what is there, and accepting it as the natural physiological byproduct of effort; you won't pay much attention to it. Don't be afraid to hurt. It's never that bad.

Of course if you are determined to look for pain in a race, you'll find it. But even then, you don't have to worry about it beforehand.

Remind yourself that it is not that bad. No matter how much you stress the limits of your body's capacity to perform and no matter how tired you get, you can deal with the discomfort and still swim fast. Certainly, it is nothing to worry about before you swim. That only gets you thinking you "have to" swim a 1500, for example, instead of how much you "want to" compete.

Racing is fun. Keep the fun in all-out efforts foremost in your mind.

Don't Be Deceived By Feel

Swimmers tend to rely too much on how they feel. Ask swimmers how they think they are going to do and more than likely they will respond by telling you how they feel.

You don't have to feel well, feel strong or feel good to swim fast. You merely have to swim fast to swim fast. If you think about it, you will probably recall that although you swam some of your best performances when you felt great, you swam others when you felt crummy and you swam some of your poorer swims when you felt great.

Don't limit how fast you swim by doubting your capability at given moments based on some subtle feelings you decided were indicative of what you do or do not have that day. Feelings are often deceptive.

Sometimes you won't feel right while warming up for a meet because the viscosity of the water differs from the pool you are used to. If you correctly conclude it feels strange because the water is more or less viscous than you are accustomed to and don't let it bother you, it's no problem. The water is the same for everyone. If you inappropriately conclude there is something wrong with you and worry about it, you're setting yourself up to swim poorly.

The feel of the water can be an important part of guiding your stroke. But don't be deceived by how well you feel or how the water feels to you.

Don't Try Too Hard

In a quest for the ultimate performance many swimmers demand of themselves the ultimate effort. Unfortunately, as a result they end up trying too hard.

You don't want to save anything. There's nothing to save it for. So, it's tempting to strive to expend every last ounce of energy, leaving you completely spent at the finish. But there is such a thing as trying too hard.

When you try too hard you end up pitting one muscle against another. You fight yourself, not allowing your muscles to work as strong, fast and fluidly as they otherwise might. And you waste a lot of energy.

The best performances will find you with a little bit left and recovering fairly rapidly, because you will have stayed relaxed in the muscles not immediately needed and used your body more efficiently. Excessive tension increases oxygen consumption and hastens muscle fatigue.

As William Paulus said reflecting on his 100 m fly victory in the 1980 Olympic Trials/National AAU's, "I just thought about swimming...relaxed. If you're tight, you can't swim well..."

An all-out sprint should not be all-out. It should be at slightly less than 100% effort. Don't try too hard.

Keep A Cool Head

Sometimes despite all your efforts to stay calm, the realization of how much a meet means to you can evoke a sudden wave of anxiety. Don't let it get the best of you. Keep a cool head. Talk sense to yourself. Tell yourself to relax and control your race.

Brian Goodell almost lost his cool in his victorious 1500 at the Montreal Olympics. But he managed to keep it together.

"I think, all of a sudden, I realized this was the Olympics. It was at the last minute, like right after warm-ups before the finals. I went in and said, 'This is for the Olympic gold. This is the race that everyone has been betting on.' There was a sudden realization that this was the big race, the one I had been shooting for for a year-and-a-half, the only thing I had been training for. I had a sudden nervousness that I had to perform here."

"I was kind of tight when I hit the water. I didn't really feel my stroke. My adenalin was flowing... I had to control myself the first couple of laps and make sure I didn't go too hard. Otherwise, I would have been dead at the end."

60

PUMP THE WELL DRY

Make A Commitment
To Do It In This Race

Many swimmers believe they can reach their goals and that someday they probably will. The trouble is they keep putting it off.

Make a commitment to do it now! Confidence in the future without confidence in the present is a false confidence, a dream that you're not bothering to make come true.

That doesn't mean you have to do it all at once. As Olympic 100 m butterfly Champion Matt Vogel says, "If you want to make the Olympics, you have to be a dreamer. Have a long-range goal and work toward that goal, but don't lose sight of your sense of realism. Take one step at a time. This way you won't get frustrated."

Take it one step at a time. But have the confidence and make the commitment to take a step now, in this race!

Make The Most Out Of Every
Opportunity. You May Never
Get Another Chance

Too many swimmers have prematurely given up on themselves and hopelessly eased up, only to unexpectedly end up on the wrong end of a close race or barely miss their goals. Others, thinking they didn't need to go any faster, have let up and cruised in to a finish, only to miss the finals or barely miss a milestone. Don't end up kicking yourself for what might have been. Make the most out of every opportunity. You may never get another chance.

Though happy with his win, following the finals of the 1980 Long Course Nationals/Olympic Trials 100 m freestyle, Rowdy

Gaines lamented just missing the world record in the prelimi-
naries. "When I went 49.6 this morning I eased up into the wall
the last 15 meters but tonight I was fighting it all the way. If I'da
known I was that close this morning I would have gone for it."

Bruce Furniss, on the other hand, seized a golden opportunity. After breaking the American Record in the 200 free in a
preliminary swim Bruce confided, "I knew I was close to the
record because I was ahead of the pack and I could hear the
crowd screaming. Really, I was just trying to qualify but I felt
good and smooth so I said, 'Why save it?'"

Don't let a good swim slip through your hands. After all, as
Bruce said, "Why save it?"

Forcefully Tell Yourself What To Do

When you are locked in the combat of competition and
milking your body for every ounce of strength, it can be tough to
keep a clear head and keep it all together, especially if your body is
screaming with the effects of pushing it to the limits. At these times
you need to talk yourself forcefully through the critical race points.

After her 1978 American Record setting National championship performance in the 1650, Sippy Woodhead said that during
the race, "I was getting dizzy, I couldn't breathe, and my
stomach was killing me from all those flip turns." But then she
began to tell herself, "Don't give up. Loosen up. Come on.
Don't tighten up."

Don't let yourself give in. Tell yourself to stay with it like
Sippy did. Even better use the discomfort as a signal to tell
yourself to pick it up.

Of course you have to be in shape to respond to that signal.
You have to have confidence in your ability to cope with the
physiological effects of effort and to successfully push through the
discomfort. The more and better you have trained, the easier it is to
have the confidence that you can pull it off. And the more you have
grooved self-talk that pushes you through the choice points in
practice, the easier it is to talk to yourself effectively in a race.

Like Sippy, Brian Goodell had the confidence to assertively talk himself through the "pain" in his 1976 Olympic 400 m freestyle victory. "I kind of said, well, here's the pain, forget it and go."

In his 1500 m victory in the same Olympics, Brian didn't let himself give up when he was behind. Instead he used vehement self-talk to ride a super last 400 to victory. "During the race the negative side of me was saying, 'You're too far behind; you can't catch them,' ... But the positive side was saying, 'Get out, get going...let go of the cookie,' which means to get your head together and just get going!"

Swim Your Own Race, Lap By Lap

If your head is busy taking a reading on how you feel and measuring where you are compared to everyone else, you can't be paying attention to your swim. Nor can you swim your best if your head is busy swimming a lap you've already completed or doing one yet to come. Concentrate on what you are doing. A race isn't a very complicated task, but it is a precarious balance of giving it all you've got without trying too hard. You have to swim efficiently and pace your race in order to cover the entire distance as fast as possible. That requires concentration.

Swim your own race, lap by lap. Bruce Furniss has had a lot of success with that strategy. He says "Basically, during the race, I just try to think about what I'm supposed to be doing out there. I really don't try to swim anyone else's race. I think about each lap as each lap and each wall as each wall."

EXPLOIT THE MAGIC WITHIN

Dare To Swim Great

You've got to believe you have as much right to win as anyone else. Don't limit your prospects of victory by believing you don't deserve it, thinking you don't have the right to win or assuming someone else is supposed to win.

No one is supposed to win! Every race is up for grabs. Victory is there for any swimmer who is willing to reach out and grab it.

That can be scary. There's safety in failure. You can't fall out of bed, if you are sleeping on the floor. But neither can you get a good night's sleep.

Accept the challenge. Dare to swim great. You have as much right to go for the gold as anyone else.

Relish Any Opportunity To Compete

A race presents a special chance to muster all your physical and psychological resources in pursuit of a singular, personally meaningful goal. A complete immersion in that quest for excellence is an unparalleled experience. It is the swimmer's ultimate high.

Mike Bruner understands. He reflects the best possible attitude when he says, "I don't care where I swim. You give me a pool and I'll try to swim my best time; I don't care if it's in Moscow or Timbuktu. I just love the sport. I just want to swim."

The Ultimate Quest

Some of you will break world records, win the Olympics, capture National titles or in other ways reap the spoils that go to the victors in competitive swimming. Most of you will not.

It may very well be, however, that the trip is more important than the destination. This volume is designed to help you swim as fast as you possibly can swim. Winning is clearly the goal of competitive swimming. It is that very quest for victory, however, that produces the rich and rewarding lifestyle of a competitive swimmer. Being totally engaged in this pursuit of excellence challenges every fiber of your being. The hope, the thrills, the exhilaration, the learning, and the excitement of the experience present the ultimate in feeling alive.

Accept the challenge. Go for the gold. You'll be richer for the quest.

Did you borrow this book? If so, why not order one for yourself?

ORDER FORM

Please send the following books by **Dr. Keith Bell**:

___ copies of **The SWIM TO WIN Playbook** .... @ $29.95 _____

___ copies of **WINNING ISN'T NORMAL** .... @ $11.95 _____

___ copies of **WHAT IT TAKES: The ABC's Of Excelling** (hardcover) .... @ $19.95 _____

___ copies of **COACHING EXCELLENCE** .... @ $19.95 _____

___ copies of **YOU ONLY FEEL WET WHEN YOU'RE OUT OF THE WATER:**
     Thoughts on Psychology and Competitive Swimming ..... @ $16.95 _____

___ copies of **TARGET ON GOLD: Goal Setting for Swimmers**
                and Other Kinds of People ..... @ $ 8.95 _____

___ copies of **CHAMPIONSHIP SPORTS PSYCHOLOGY** .... @ $21.95 _____

___ copies of **RELAXATION TRAINING (Audio Tape)** .... @ $11.95 _____

___ copies of **The Nuts & Bolts of PSYCHOLOGY FOR SWIMMERS** .... @ $11.95 _____

                          SUBTOTAL _____

      Sales Tax: Please add 6.25% sales tax for every book shipped to a Texas address. _____

      SHIPPING & HANDLING
      For single copy orders or first book please include $4.00. $4.00 ____
____ additional copies of **The SWIM TO WIN Playbook** please add $3.00 per copy. _____
____ additional copies of all other titles please add $1.00 per copy. _____
____ number of copies being shipped outside the USA * please <u>add</u> $5.00 per copy. _____
      * Please remit International Money Order or check drawn off U.S. bank in U.S. dollars.

                  Total for SHIPPING & HANDLING _____

                ## TOTAL ENCLOSED _____

NAME _____

ADDRESS _____

CITY _____ **STATE** _____ **ZIP** _____

PHONE _____

EMAIL _____

Make checks payable and send to: **KEEL PUBLICATIONS**
                                  P.O. Box 160155
                                Austin, Texas 78716
                      512-327-1280 / swimpair@flash.net

Please allow approximately 3 weeks for delivery

Contact us for wholesale & quantity prices.